Poems of love from my time

Cover Design by Cheikh B. Dramé.

ISBN: 978-0-557-14591-1

Extended Autobiography:

Second born child of the family and son of Papa Sette Drame and Fatoumata Dembele, I am born on July 7, 1984 at Dakar, Senegal (West Africa).

I studied first at an Elementary Public School at Mabo. My mother is a professor and is my first teacher both theoretically and academically since I sat in her classroom all the way to the 5th grade. Then, I moved to the capital to start Junior High School. My academic performance has always been ranked between the five best of my classes.

Nevertheless, I didn't stop trying to give honor to my only dream, which is to serve people. That fire kept burning within, although it may be obscured at some time, it was still there. It is the desire to reach my full potential.

I have received unlimited prizes and awards from the seventh grade to the ninth grade. After getting a certificate to have finished the secondary school, I moved to New York (USA) in August 2000. Having problems to integrate in an American school basically because of the English language. Then I migrated to an immigrant school and three months later, I was at Taft High School, in the Bronx. There, I participated in a lot of organizations and community services, and after a discovery of my writing talent, I was nominated student of the month on March 2001. I never stop about helping my school, that I have joined the Mediator team, which was needy in a school of violence.

Despite my math teacher, Mr. Bleeker, who wanted me to stay for another year; I graduated in January 2002 at the age of 17.

From then on, I went to CUNY, Borough of Manhattan Community College, to earn my Associate's degree in Computer Science. At graduation, I received the Dean's list honor.
The next stop was Queens College. And in August 2007, I received my BA.
And the Saga continues...

Dedicated
To all the lovers around the world.

Dedicated
To my 2 sisters: Adja and Sokhna Drame and to my brother: Ousmane Drame

Acknowledgments

I would like to thank my high school English teacher at Taft High School (in the Bronx).
I would like to extend my gratitude to all my classmates and friends who gave me positive feedback, which encouraged me to publish it for the enjoyment of all the people around the world. Among them is Philip Parzygnat.

Poems of love from my time

Cheikh Bamba Drame,
The prince of words

8

Contents

*In the farm of my father where I
cultivated poems under the
oppressive sun; those poems that I
take until now at the time of
dinner, make me remember the
delicious times.*

Poems of Love

By the loving flame that burns my heart,
I approve of you in all sincerity,
with your sparkling smile,
your spaced teeth marking the symbol of love,
graceful steps deprived of any tiredness,
and I am in love.

You, my Negress,
the woman of all pains of which,
I would love to huddle the night.
Without you,
my life is nothing,
as the illiterate who crosses life as a blind man.

To only see you,
nothing than a handshake,
makes me appease hunger and thirst
like loneliness.
With the sense of Funa-Na,
I think of the cornice: dark blue
sky with its high mountains,
you belong to me.

I love you with power,
but with reason.

Thus always growing towards new
shores,
in the night carried without return,
couldn't we throw sparks of love in
this river only one day?
I think of this night we will go out
and I will say to it:
"go slower and the dawn will
dissipate the night."

The morn,
blooming of all the flowers,
not of the day;
you transpierced my heart by an
infernal light.
This light,
born of an instinct of second,
formed part of the unknown secrecy
of affection.
That dazzling light was also felt by

Romeo and Juliet.

I will bring a sufficient praise so
that your bosom is trustful.

Under the beats slowed down,
my heart pants.
I breathe with difficulty,
hot air throws out of my mouth like
spittles of a volcano:
my love for you is so strong that it
weakens me.

I love you,
I love you,
and I need to tell you that.
And that is my heart that is dying
to inform you.

Dumb man with my pains,
quiet with my nerves,
underhand with my desires,
and I still moan of love and sorrow
for not being with you.
It is toward you that I lean again,
my love,
light of my mind and heart.

I think of Hollywood,
with its arranged mountains,
which is the reflection of an
amorous destination.

A gallant history is born between
you and me.

Do not look at me anymore like eyes
of a friend;
forget the relations of friendships,
think of the love that will change
your life.

Love is an unknown fire that
confines itself inside a soul.

I am insane with your body;
I know it well not to be afraid of
it.

Do not smile at me anymore,
because your smile is devastating,
not to say ransacked.
Do not direct toward me your
tendering eyes anymore,
because your charm is irresistible,
trying, enticing, tyrannical.

I am waiting for your answer but not
your language.
I speak to you about feelings; you
excavate me with your eyes;
I defy your language but not your
mouth.

When I looked at the range, the
rain, the sky;

it is about you that I meditated.
You are the mysterious woman that I
dreamed since always.

The rain falls on our world.
These blue, benevolent and valorous
clouds block the sun.
Rendered dumb by these winds of
humors,
infatuated people are drowned in;
while your beauty makes me
prosperous.

Our meeting was not random,
because pricked by your generosity
at school:
I met you in winter,
from this moment,
my favorite season.

You are the goddess of all beauties
and you rule queen in my heart.
I don't know how to design you or to
locate you,
because you are bewitching.
Yes, you are!
You are the princess of my passion
and without you nothing will fill.

I love you,
that is why I do not want your eyes
to become victims,
staring at other boys.

Soft and plaintive angel who speaks while signing,
where your handshake tickles me,
and your extreme glance transpierces my heart like each lightning.

I love you strongly in my heart.

I switch off like a candle when I feel your breath behind me.
I shiver of passion when I am beside you.
I feel a different heat, attracting, in you;
and that, that is the difference.
It shows a visible love.

You opened my eyes.
Now, I see the world through the eyes of love.
And everything is beautiful,
nothing like I have ever experienced before.
You offered me the opportunities to see differently
for I was a blind man since birth.

In life, it is to love, or to be loved.
Let me cherish you for I have the rights to love you
and you have the duties to accept

me.

The dogs that bark,
The lion that reigns,
The sheep that grazes,
The tree that protects,
The cricket that sings the drill,
In general, all says: "I am once fond of someone."

I would be a beggar with your oath.
I am your slave with your covetousness.
I would follow you until the end of the world.
I am with you, you should not doubt about me.

I give you my arm,
can I give you a heart that adores you?
You retain my heart, my spirit,
perhaps it is Destiny who is responsible for this.

The carnal communion cannot be without the acceptation of the bosom.
Then, at least try to follow your enthusiasm,
but not the stupidities.

Do not divert me clean of the love

that I have for you.
Do not say to me to suffer in silence.
Love is a disease and I am afraid that I have caught it.

I am insane of your body,
and I would like to be there with the depths of this winter so chilly.
I want to emerge in your exotic body.
I want to be embedded in your inland sea.

Despite everything your eyes did not notice me, cruel!

Torn heart by your wish,
begs by your will,
requests by despair the leniency of your feelings.

When I would while liking,
received of you the gifts of your prowess's,
this MUSE promised,
I would devote them to the loves of Louie the 3rd,
lovers and the in-love ones from time immemorial are friendly.

I love you;
I repeat it with envy.

Because Affection is dangerous:
it hides, deceives, simulates and
dissimulates at the same time.
For that it is necessary to show
loving, to pass behind the mirror,
to give up on the bank the beauty,
the elegance, the nonchalance.

Passion is the universe of
appearances, a lure, a trap.
It is necessary to taste them,
undergo happiness and the pains.

A lack of self-confidence,
sometimes a blindness on my real
desires,
and yet a hesitation to engage.

Series of choices are opened for
you.
Again friend of kindnesses and
promises,
and in spite of that, the concern
for not being liked.

I will remove you of your torments,
the problems,
the drudgeries, and the
embarrassments.
But, moreover contradictions of a
woman does not disturb me.
Love is the instrument,
which makes it possible to dominate

contradictions,
to transgress limits, and to
reconcile opposites.

The beauty vibrates behind the
polish of the mirror.
And the woman should not refuse to
sacrifice her youth.

I will change style into changing
softness.

Love sowed the disorder in the
universe of my words and things.
I follow the world by circumventing
it.
I drain the feeling, I start to take
part in nature;
I am a pulled up horse that escapes
from the obstacle.
I pass to dimensions;
I reveal it to you while wanting
elucidating.

The wise ones sometimes,
in spite of their wisdom,
turn their back to God.

Events in events,
love continues, passes stages,
exceeds maintained contradictions,
reconsiders its steps, supplements,
insists, refutes, and succeeds.

We are in an age where the funs and
the plays are allowed to the
children.
But we must give some of our
thoughts, as serious reflexions.

Love is a so natural and all seems
so pleasant.
Because what can one wish more
without love?
But as it is a quite pleasant
spectacle for the universe to thus
see believing as two humanoids love
each other in the madness.

To tell you, I hasten to come to
you,
and in addition with the truths that
I said to you than this one:
I am a single man, humble, and
faithful.
Sincerities, the slogans as well as
the proverbs,
and the lies contain truths, which
can be used as lessons.

All speaks in my text—my statements
and even the commas.
I use animals to learn how to like.
I will keep you up with less
adventure,
to trace in these lines, slight

paintings.

My name is Cheikh Drame.
I am, by right, a good boy. I want to be meaningful in your life.
Entrust to me your problems and the remedies will come.
In another way, one sees better than his next.
Whoever saw much, can have retained much.
One day will come, which is not far, to spread my name.
And we believe the correctness only when it occurs.

Love without having rivals.

Do not put in your spirit for most beautiful of the world.
Do not blame the mirrors to be real.
Living more than content in your major error,
the mirror: isn't it a stupidity of others?
Perhaps the luxury and the madness swelled your treasure.
The praises tickles and gains the spirits.
The favors of a nice girl are the price.

I fear of speaking to you, but not

the unease.

Your body appears to me in marvelous
state;
you will definitely be a perfect
companion.

Believe me on word that I want to
drive out this love away from me,
but when I close the gate by the
nose,
it returns by the window.

Early or late, you must trust a man.
Why not to begin with me!

Your attractions are used as grace
of model.
Could you be favorable to the
innocent plays of the body with
body?

Love is a strange master;
happy is one who can know it.

My heart is even smitten by you,
plugged.
Love, Love, Love, when you hold us;
one can say: "Goodbye Prudence."
The pure-love plugs the spirits.

Love is not a tale with invented
pleasure.

And like one day, the winds
retaining their breath,
peacefully let approach their
vessels;
I discover you, my sweetheart.
I am using the truth,
to show by experiment,
a kiss when it is ensured,
will make the present situation
change.

And it is necessary to be satisfied
with its condition and reality;
to the consulting of the sea of
Happiness, Wisdom:
we must close the ears;
for those who will join in,
the sea promises miracles and
wonders.
After, the tenderness and well-being
will come.
Then, let's unite by the light of
love.

Each day that I look at you,
your beauty grows in front of my
eyes.
You oblige me to tell you the word
that,
like the night and the day, makes me
dream:
it is the junction of your heart and

mine.
Thoughts in front of our future,
oblige me to think of the greatest
feast of tomorrow,
and that our fruits will fall one
day.

Oh! My adored, think with less of
the future.
I do not promise much,
but what I say will never come out
of the wind.

I am insane of you.
Your Beauty, it is properly a charm;
it returns my heart attentive,
or rather it holds me captive.
I am attracted by your infinite
beauty.
Love leads to its liking, the hearts
and the spirits.

Give me love, where my heart has
fun.

The time, which destroys all,
respecting our love,
will let me cross the years and its
difficulties in this life.

It is from you that my poems await
their entire price.

Everything is glare in your body
even in the unnoticeable parts.

Words and glances, all is charm on
your premise.
Protect from now on, the word,
Amour.
After all that, don't I deserve to
be the only man in your life?

If I were king of the world, I would
build palaces only for you,
because one does not owe a wish
according to any truth.

Some oeuvre of art, all of that
shouts: "Love is miraculous. "

Any man lies, but in each lie, there
are some truths.
And when I speak of love,
it is always the veracity because
nobody dallies,
nor plays with it.

But whatever, similar moments will
never return,
it is a chance that is necessary to
take by the hair.

And when I meditate:
is it necessary to possess many
objects so soft and charming at the

expense of my unsatisfied Self;
won't I feel any more charm which
stops me?
Have I surpassed the age to love?

I am extremely and strongly fond of you; I am in love; I am enamored of you. And if love doesn't give a relish to the pleasures that Hymen gives us, I do not see that we are better. I would desire to say more, but the words were lost in my throat. I want that you believe me. I am in the age of reason.

Goodbye's Letter

Look at your beauty by the window.
The moldiness will replace the perfume.

In the middle of winter,
Whereas the flowers will open out,
For you they will fade away.
You are in the summer,
your beauty scintillating but not eternally.
Your beauty will tarnish,
As the iron which corrodes under the contact with air.

At least to repeat, my heart will go to more its wishes,
to warn you.

Tempting does not mean to be liked.

Color, skin, teeth;
aren't you a girl after all?
Weren't you born to be liked?
Or, your mirror has misled you by
making you pass for the prettiest.
You are perfect!

Let your feelings carry you,
but not your beauty.
To sell one's beauty is dangerous.
You will receive in exchange only
the fortune which will be followed
by the problems.

To you, my beautiful.

Hidden Feelings to the Sacred Woman

When shall I see you again, the pure
love on your face.

Every summer time sets your blazing
beauty--
the golden riddle of your smile.

Oh! Love! I can understand now its
language.
The language of the pure love that
runs in my veins.

When the lamp takes refuge from the
top of the hill,
I saw the brightness of your dark
beauty:
pearls like stars on your chest.

I sing your immense beauty that
cannot set my mind free.

Your eyes in hot summer nights are

like stars.

Oh! I sing your calm beauty behind
the gates.
That is why I tremble in your
presence,
your love is burning me inside.

Loneliness has caught me in cause of
your inattention.

Everyday I sing,
but no sign of your appearance.
Maybe I am just hallucinating.
Maybe you never hear my language –
the pure language of love.

God knows my pain is real.
I have nothing to prove but tears
and songs.

I am a slave to you by an unknown
pain.
Maybe, the loyal wind will
communicate it to you.
Maybe, back, the wind will leave me
with the silence.

Oh! My dear strange lover! Are you
real!
It is that haunting smile that hunts
my mind and in the meantime,
an unknown feeling runs through my

body.

I am so lonely--loneliness beyond my
power of expression.

It is my fault that I have looked at
you.
Now, my mind is prisoner of
memories –the sickness of my heart.
You are so real in my dreams.

Oh, Angel! I shall sing your grace,
your beauty eternally.

I have learned what Love is,
but never what is sufferance.

A word from your mouth could choke
me.
You are the source of my life.
You are the reason of my living.
I can't realize how lonely I was
before I met you.

Every word, out of my mouth,
is limpid as the water fountain and
real as heaven.

I haven't felt anything yet but
sufferance.

Oh! "goddess of the beauties";
deliver me!

Still sufferance in my heart,
with no expression.
Another anonymous pain, painful
beyond words.
I don't now what I am becoming.
Who knows?

By the loving flame that burns my
heart,
I approve of you in all sincerity,
with your sparkling smile,
your spaced teeth marking the symbol
of love,
graceful steps deprived of any
tiredness,
and I am in love.
I declare it to you. I am in love.

I am scared of losing this sweet
fruit,
which is ready to fall down.
This sweet fruit, ready, surely to
grow on her own.

Your love is the only thing that can
satisfies the hungry soul that I am.

I am jailed in a sufferance camp.

I do not know what love is,
but I love you.
I love you so much,
I am blind to the world I am living.

Believe to the words out of my
mouth.
That nothing comes out,
but only truth.

I am lashing with pure iced words.
That I ask in return,
only understanding.

Toward traveling in your soul,
discovering new things I would never
dare,
exploring new feelings,
later challenging myself.
Scariness?
Ok!
No more!

Now, baby!
I am revealing the dark hidden
feelings that I have for you,
my sacred woman.

I am so thirsty that only your love
can appease my thirst.

I am lost in the world that is not
mine.
Just being in the deepest dream,
but crazy to think you feel the
same.
Just crazy of not having the hand of

the subject,
and of which is unknown to my
imagination.

Dream is the second world of one who
is not satisfied.
There I am!
Still dreaming of the day we will be
together.

I still remember, me and you,
always looking at each other,
but no exchanged words.
I wish you could feel my love.
And if it is true from you, to feel
the same.
The feeling that we can still share
our love,
sends a breeze throughout my body.
To make you appreciate the truth,
you are the elite of my heart.

I am suffering slowly,
because you never paid attention to
me.
Always when I try to come up to you,
you don't seem interested.
That repulsion is killing me.
I am like a fool.
I feel like an idiot just to pretend
that you feel the same.

I am sleepy—restless heart and full

of hope.
I feel abandoned, thirsty for love.

You are the queen of my dreams.

Also, the light in your heart,
shows me the way.
Show me the meaning of feeling
lonely.

Yet, I can't understand why we can't
be together.
Yet more, why do I suffer in the
forgotten world?
Damn,
love is crazy.
People must say,
I have lost my reason.

Sad Lover.
I can't realize why it is so.
Tell me that you feel the same.
Again, inspiring my heart,
confusing my mind,
adored heart taken by foolishness;
the consequences are:
To say that I was living.
To see that I was lonely.

I am sorry of not getting together
with you.
Should I talk to the wall?
Certainly not.

Who should I address to?
To show that love I am so scared to unveil.

Throughout the world,
we see many faces, cultures, making us different from each other,
but not better.
Love is what transgresses appearances.
Love is for people who see no limits.

Concentrate before you act,
calm down before you talk,
speechless of feared people.
Yet the desire to be understood.

My pen, on the paper,
even cries, scratches on it,
couldn't understand these symbols
that can only relate with hearts.

I am sorry is not an excuse but a terrible mistake to have sent my heart in the unknown world.

Yet still, I want you in these remarkable moments that separate us, and the deep feeling that constrains me in the inside.

Why are the stars looking at me?

This beautiful moon of a delice
night,
walked away in a regrettable chance
that we could be ensemble,
side by side,
glancing to the sparkling little
rayons of the river,
a kiss down inside,
lungs full of air;
a heart lives again.

This is the way I express myself,
through words that go along with the
wind,
in a coherent manner that lets my
nose breathes music.
Let it go so I could relax
painstakingly of the restless mind
and spirit.
Sadness comes to recomfort me.
I am happy now.

The Sun will rise. It can't always be raining. So, must I rise every day to give this day its due.

www.ingramcontent.com/pod-product-compliance
Ingram Content Group UK Ltd.
Pitfield, Milton Keynes, MK11 3LW, UK
UKHW020216250726
13967UKWH00001B/17

9 780557 145911